SOUTHERN SEASON

SOUTHERN SEASON

Alice Moser Claudel

Foreword by

Richard Harter Fogle

English Professor of the University of North Carolina

Pikeville College Press
of the
APPALACHIAN STUDIES CENTER
Pikeville, Kentucky

iii

Blue and Gray Press

CONTENTS

ACKNOWLEDGMENTS

We are grateful to the editors and owners of the following publications for permission to reprint the poems. The volumes and pages are given after each poem:

American Poet
Beloit Poetry Journal
Carolina Quarterly
Colorado Quarterly
Descant
Epos
Experiment
Folio
Furioso
Matrix
New Mexico Quarterly Review
Nimrod
North Carolina Folklore
Pebble
Poem
Poet
Prairie Schooner
Quarterly Review of Literature
Shenandoah
South
Southern Literary Messenger
Southern Poetry Review
Tramp
Three Lyric Poets
University of Kansas City Review
University of Houston Forum

FOREWORD

This is the work of a distinguished mind—and as a surly, easily-bored old English teacher, I do not go around talking about my students' distinguished minds without, let us say, extreme provocation. (I am able to claim Mrs. Alice Claudel as a student, though in poetry it would be much more appropriate for me to sit at *her* feet.) These catch the wonder of ordinary things. One seizes upon a single phrase from "City Carnival" to describe their total effect: "this magic square/ Sharp-etched," which is a distillation of Mrs. Claudel's gift. Her poetry is sharply outlined, distinctly visual. But it reaches outward and beyond toward rich implications, toward something unattainable that is based on the firmly attained. To put the case perhaps too abstractly, she writes about the timelessness in time, the limitless in bounded space.

Her "Autumn Walk," for instance, can make us think at once of Keats and T. S. Eliot in its "drama lost on time's dry wind/ Arrested for the savoring." It has another quality, too, for these are poems, though the self in them is unobtrusive, of self-discovery. The poet is in her poems, but as an added dimension, or further irradiation in their picturing.

These are the generalities of Mrs. Claudel's poetry, but each of her poems has its unique life; in each of them something happens that is individual. "Tulane's Night Biology Class" is a case in point: a beating egg heart, susceptible of many and impressive interpretations, is the center of attention. But the meaning "earns itself," as Robert Penn Warren might say, from a particularity that is somehow its own guarantee, and goes beyond itself to pervade the whole experience.

> The tear that trembled
> On my own light's rim
> Was more in fear than sorrow
> For the doctor's gem:
> A pounding heart,
> Glassed in a cup,
> An endless whim.

These poems are experiences, genuine, living perceptions. We would all get these effects if we could, no doubt, but to achieve them takes technique: the composing hand and eye, restraint, a sense of true proportion. Mrs. Claudel is often masterly in relating the parts of her scenes to achieve an intense unity. To present a final example, in "Lee Circle" she manages an effect that is both startling and just, by looking outward from the statue and its grounds to the encircling streets, full of motion and sound. The remote becomes the near, the actual is transformed in aesthetic distance to a magically suspended and timeless moment, a concrete symbol perfected beyond accident.

Richard Harter Fogle

Chapel Hill, North Carolina
November 27, 1971

FOR LACK OF RHYME

"He is not delicate," I said,
    "And does not know the feel of subtlety";
But I have seen him look in other eyes
    For something he has never found in me.

Time murders dreams and cautious dreamers clip
    The wings of thoughts until they walk in words.
So he who only knows my ways in speech
    Would never guess that I have thoughts like birds,

Warm and sweet and colorful as glass
    That catches all the summer in its shine;
For my love looks in eyes of blue and brown
    For visions he has never found in mine.

So he must choose. I wish that I were wise
    Instead of sad. Perhaps then I would see
My love is not immune to poetry
    But longs for lyrics never found in me.

From *Southern Literary Messenger*
    Vol. IV, No. 9
    Summer, 1942

WHITE

I walked down a long street
Whose doors were dark, white-wreathed,
In an old movie of remembrance,
So I stepped softly on the city sidewalk
As though it were clay I knew
Covered with leaves in a great triangle
Shielded with white walls
Where leaves kept falling, falling
From friendly trees whose guard
Was a nut-brown gnome, a blue-eyed crone.
The wreaths stared like accuser's eyes
At my heart alive on a tenement street
Where children's songs were killed
By a plague whose sepulchres are white
Mourned by white wreaths
The eyes dropping dry leaf tears.

From *University of Houston Forum*
(Fall, 1970)

THE PRISONER

However she goes, she is islanded always
By this deep sea that welled from childhood's fears.
An ardent earth can never choke its waters,
Immune to suns of the invading years.

Sometimes she leans where other worlds loom warmly
To find a light where any boat might go,
But whispers seaweed on the furtive football
And fog enfolds the word she may not know.

Furioso
Vol. II, No. 1
1943

NIGHT ON THE RIVER

The moon burns on this rich and midnight tide,
Fringed by small diamonds and three rubies at
                                        its side,
But this small boat, immune to charms,
Rolls in the river's siren-arms . . .
Where years ago, De Soto slipped,
Boxed and burnished, solemn-lipped.
The pearls that were De Soto's eyes
Will never rise
But our light falls on night that is
A moving dark no less than his.

From *Three Lyric Poets*
(Edited by Alan Swallow)

I REMEMBER

The Lafitte House, a lazy record playing
An Intermezzo, and myself (breathless with you) saying,
"All ladies should be lovely as the Viennese.
"How sad that velvet patches are no more the fashion
With women," and our hands met in a timeless passion,
Playing their private melodies.

So we sat there till dawn, till the swallows sang,
While the old Cathedral bell rang
Five . . . and then we started
Down the shrouded street to my home.
Your voice talked plain words, but your face spoke Rome.
My thoughts were conquered and we parted.

Then, everywhere, salon or cabaret,
Or the French Market (for *cafe au lait*)
I heard the Intermezzo in a fever
Of fear, joy or as a dash
Of icy water, for the pulse was rash,
Crying, "Love this Imperator forever!"

Here is my book. It cools the mind
That rages. Nostalgia will find
New ways to die, for it is almost
Nothing to hear the records play
Intermezzo and nothing that you look away.
And I mourn not the you I found, but one I lost.

From *Southern Literary Messenger*
    Vol. IV, No. 9
    September, 1942

RIVERSIDE DRIVE

Sometimes this Drive
Holds almost the world's weight
In metallic people
And what they desire . . .
Jewels and furs, the eyes
Of burning courtesans
And the fuel for their fire,
The fierce luxury
Of cars from Italy,
And sleek houses
That rise disdainfully
Above the dark of the river.
And it holds the statues
Of very great men,
Their stone eyes filled with pride.
It holds so much—this drive . . .
That even a shabby poet,
Who has never prophesied,
Absorbed in the sunset's red,
Is alarmed to feel
A tremor beneath his feet
Lest it collapse with a roar!

The Tramp
Fall, 1940

GOING HOME

River water's the magnet
draws us home
that once carried us off
in selfmade weather
from the monotony of place
whose names we knew
and names we bore
when legendary winds
ruffled the mind.
The city sprawls now
in a later sun,
a cat whose charms we know.
We need old names,
who lose the names we bear
to tell us where we are.
The river draws us there.

Folio
Volume VI, number 1
Summer, 1970

HOW

When Death's deep eye is fixed on me,
How shall I, hunted, find a cave
Where my storm can still blow free
From anonymous silence of the grave?

From *Three Lyric Poets*

A WALK IN THE DARK

The cars slide like shining fish
Past the window of a stare,
And one who held the world within,
Feels it slipping, scene by scene
Out of all adjusted space
And pigeon-holes the mind contains.
Not the tongues of wise old heads
Or dreaming conjured out of time
Are glue to put them back in place.
It is too late to rearrange
Shifting skies in patterns set.
Fix the eye for surging change.

From *Three Lyric Poets*

JACKSON SQUARE

(New Orleans)

Block within giant block,
Like an oriental game, the Square
Sits, teasing thought with
Geometric beauty . . . everywhere

Haunts us, who ride the furious
Steel stallions of our day,
To return here where floatsam
And the hungry sprawl or pray,

And madness mellows under ordered age.
Cabildo, Church, and Presbyter
Triumph like music, and time
Sleeps in the Square.

War seems a frantic ghost;
For puffing ferries and the river-horns
Woo the air gently . . .

Above the jade lawns
Andrew Jackson rides, hat in hand,
As blithely real against the grey sky
As peddlers with their fragrant wares.
The cat-eared spires and the street-lamp's eye

Warm the boats that crowd the river's
Side with a strange peace.
A bell drops evening softly
On soldiers now at ease.

And what if Jackson's hand
Is raised to cheer
(Since we blaze to freedom side by side)
The booted English he once battled here?

From *Southern Literary Messenger*
Volume IV, No. 9
September, 1942

A LADY ON THE DESIRE CAR

"A transfer to the Metairie Bus,"
The Creole lady said,
Tilting her head arrogantly.
And settled her skirt and feet
Below the window seat.
She turned her antique ring subtly
To show it cost more than anything of ours,
And the street-cars rolled through Frenchtown,
Past the cobble-stones and spires
Of her ancestral sires.
Poverty will not betray
What her eyes and gestures say,
Till Death more debonair
Outwits the haughiest stare
With his impervious air
That, like a soothing balm,
Makes all commotion calm.

New Mexico Quarterly Review
Volume XII, No. 1
February, 1942

THE FALL OF A HOUSE

It seems so strange
To see a house brought down
Like a hunted creature,
Buckling at the knees;
The geometric pattern broken
And rooms, once vital,
Harried by the breeze.
Silent . . . the cats come home
And no one knows,
Seeing their troubled eyes,
What of their old world
In these battered bricks
They still surmise.

From *Three Lyric Poets*
(edited by Alan Swallow)

POEM 1

Hold the day—unwind the hour
Back to the furled flower,
Back to the eager eye
That saw a guileless smile within
And not the gall upon the skin.
If minute curled on minute gain
The fragile soul a wrap of pain,
Was it that the gaze was bent
The way the days went?
Or that the unsuspecting must
Earn acid drink and dream of dust?

From *Three Lyric Poets*

OLD GIROD STREET CEMETERY

Waxen white magnolia blooms,
White oleanders overhead
Drop their round fresh petals on
The white squares of the dead.
The grass teems with whispering
Of creatures in a stranger-world.
Black and green they leap
Across the terraces of sleep.

In the warmth and the peace,
In eternal flowing tides
Like a river, green and white . . .
Falls the shadowed city light.

Neo-Grecian braves a sky
The railroad warehouse dominates
As a special toy of breath.
A lute worked out in iron lace
Makes the music for
Silent-footed death.

O, "loved and honored, widely mourned,"
We mourn those who wept for you.
The scorpion and the buttercup
Take their patrimony up.

From *New Mexico Quarterly Review*
      Summer, 1943
      Vol. XIII, No. 2

Reprinted in the volume *Best Poems of 1943*
      selected and edited by Alan Swallow

Also used by Leonard Huber for the frontispiece
      to his book *Of Glorious Immortality*

MAGAZINE STREET

(New Orleans)

A long and tired street,
Wearing small business of the Irish and the Dutch
Stole with artless ease
The lacework balconies
Of savoir-faire Creoles.
  The bakery, whose magic smell
  Revives frail memory,
The pharmacy, with ruby red
And cobalt urns of glass,
And Cleopatra just around a dream,
Have lights that huddle,
Chattering in their doom.
The streetcar rolls across Victorian age
Where porticoes of swift delight,
And gingerbread, assail the sight.
Poydras Asylum for the Protestants,
Sensible and white,
Xavier University, nunlike in the night,
For the eruditely black,
Look forward
And three-quarters back . . .
While we thunder onward
Swallowing the sky's long light.
  A snowball stand with jewel syrups
  Gleaming in the jars,
The glazed magnolia trees
Have time to pause . . . the wheels rush on.
Boy on the corner, dreaming to the moon,
The undertaker's shop
Is X to you, your briefest thought
Ignores this dusty symbol
On a dying street.

From *Matrix*
Fall, 1943, No. 1

A SOUTHERN MEMORY

War, I think, has finally pawned Death's crown,
His singular dignity
Lost in plurality.
And lovers of pomp
Though alive to the shade
Of his once-imperial shadow
Feel poor.
The myths of Death in his prime
Once fixed the flags of time.
Mixed in any crowd,
Among cattle driven to market,
The dead glide now
In caravans of simonized sedans
Through zones of every imagined toll.
They are the subjects
Sown on acres of paper,
Their king no longer a lightning
Lashing the placid sky
And leaving a fearsome image on the eye.
We are part of what we see.

Still through the curtains of childhood
Pageants roll,
Even seeming burlesque of dignity
The warmest advocate of ceremony.
I remember a hearse
And its horses weeded in black,
Sharp as sentences on the summer air.
Black mourners shuddered.
Their shuffling steps, the muffled drums,
The cadenced moaning
Testified love had changed.
Like a visible dirge
The thin black men
Bent with their purple ribbons
That hung to the ground,
And the growing numbers

Sighed with each funereal sound.
When the grieving surged back home,
The corpse was gone.
The jaunty trumpets ribalded heaven's throne.
"Didn't he ramble? Didn't he ramble?"
Stuffing their ears with sound
To drown the bone.
Wasn't there time to dance
And time to savor?
"He rambled till the Butcher cut him down!"

From *Experiment*

OUTSIDE

Outside the thin tissue of remembering
Travels the world whose pain we ached to cure.
"We shall rub it with youthful balm and blood,
In eternity of living make a permanence of good!"
But cosmic pain and general rage diminish
With the lengthening breath . . .
The Joan of Arc shrugged secondary
To the belief in death.
It is too late to stalk a terror.
Give me the sunlight
Though my indignation's swept
Into the dustbin of forgotten nights.
I have erased the little weeping children.
I have ignored the pressure of man's hell
And cannot see the shadows on the sun
Only my own grief in a private well.

Quarterly Review of Literature
Volume 1, No. 1
Autumn, 1943

(Now edited at Princeton,
by the same editor, Theodore Weiss,
Poet-in-Residence at Princeton)

DRYADES STREET ON SATURDAY NIGHT

St. John's Steeple, Byzantine,
Sharpens the semi-tropic scene

In which dark, angular girls
Flare bright jackets and steamed curls.

The undulating throng makes
Loud patterns, congeals, and breaks,

Moving past patient, Semite beards,
Weighing and counting, measuring yards

Of sleazy silks and cheap brocade.
An onyx doorman buys gold braid

And on the corner there
A tree lets fall its emerald hair

Like a clown's permanent wave
Over a billboard. The eye is slave

To raucous color now, for it flows
Animated, fabricated, and the heart goes

Wild with new rhythms. The mind closes
And the pores breathe magnolias and black roses

While the statue of St. John's, mild and sweet,
Unwavers like the sky on a moving street.

From *American Poet*
    and the volume *Three Lyric Poets*
    (Edited by Alan Swallow)

ABOVE THE RIVER

Above the Mississippi, ten stories high,
Remote and closer still, the streets lie.
The walking eye sees merely panoply;
Itself; and brief chicanery.
Only the smell of tar, nostalgic and intense,
Rises here to lull the clear sense
Of streets my fathers knew
Whose surly ebb and flow
The furtive guess explores . . .
From a lost black barouche going
Along the river's edge, the crimson cars flowing
Among frail waves of dust.
Now, greatness is a word wrested
Out of whispering past.
Sullen buildings boxed along the river's side
Hold little of dreaming and less of pride.
Yet time sifted beyond sense was not romance
But form and tone and variance
Lost to arthritic days. Spires
And cobalt skies poise above desires
Of men accepting shapes, packaged & prescribed.
Here thoughts overtake hours & space & Death
The watchman, pounding
Against the doors of breath,
His silent knocking sounding
Above the river-horns, the siren-speech of trains,
Colliding cars and whistles. This explains
Nothing of what lies before one
Who blends the centuries with the present eyes.

From *Three Lyric Poets*
(Edited by Alan Swallow)

EVENING

Now in the heavy dusk
Safe in the ice-cream parlour's box of light,
I see myself go in and out with cones,
Their rapturous goodness keen along my tongue;
The half-forgotten forms of little girls,
All me, and conjured by this chair
Fairy-like and special for a child.
Ireland's faces limned across the air,
Leaning above the windows,
Make the moment real.
And one takes orders patiently,
Who does not guess the way I feel,
Deep in her own world's lonely ways.
While I am new and looking at the night
With one girl's eyes
Whose waist her love's arm strays.
How marvelously scent returns
The fled scenes to a present sense
And all the hour's necessity
Loses its bright significance,
Becomes but one ring
On a strand of light
Around the cool throat of eternity.

From *Three Lyric Poets*
   (Edited by Alan Swallow)

CHALMETTE

(Site of the Battle of New Orleans)
No sound alarms this river-bordered earth,
Except the oak-trees' imperceptible growth
And hum of lazy tropic insects . . .
No sharpness stabs the breath with sudden beauty
Of strident radiant flowers on green isles,
Or silent snow upon a sleeping hill,
But brown this warm earth lies,
Open and patient under steady sun.

From *American Poet*
Vol. II, Number 10
January, 1943

OUR TIME

Lady Macbeth's dreams were sweet
Compared with fears that haunt our time
When the puzzle that was almost pieced
Bursts into the alien air
Like shrapnel, falling somewhere
Beyond the framework of the mind.
Sometimes the dazed dreamer clutches
Old myths, lest he go careening, too,
But the implacable nightmare's moral
Prods him loose to reel again:
One fights knowingly, or blows
With the wind, makes fertile the earth
With death, or building fresher worlds
Storms the defense of cruelty and pain.

From *Matrix*
Vol. 4, No. 1
Spring, 1942

PATIENT IN CHARITY HOSPITAL

The technician seems a god
To her, staring.
"How many seconds to snap a picture
Of a rush case? She has a fever 104 degrees!"
How many seconds to snap a heart?
"Be quiet," he says to the unreal face,
"Don't breathe . . . don't move . . ."
White an opiate for the eye
While shadows of the room
Hang, then crowd.
A history, compact in this face,
Waits for the clinic girl to pull its chart.
"Hold your breath, now. Don't breathe."
One stenographer knows fear
Like a thousand knives,
And the skies outside the walls are grey.
"No use to take the X-ray," says the technician,
"The woman is dead. Call her ward
Far a carrier. Get ready for the next case.
Her number was 128-368,
No radiograph taken."
"Hold your breath, now. Don't move,
Don't breathe."

From *Three Lyric Poets*
(Edited by Alan Swallow)

SCENE ONE

"I wonder how my hair looks,"
She worried as she sat
Beside him at the cinema,
"And if he likes my hat.

"Should I be light and laughing
Or subtle, or demure . . .
Just a little hesitant
Or confidant and sure?

"Or should I try to show him
The essence that is Me,
The one I groped so hard to find
Through dark and agony?"

While calmly he accepted her
As part of his own scene
And let his thoughts wander with
The lovers on the screen.

From *Three Lyric Poets*

NOCTURNE

Windward
We flung ourselves,
The winter night
Sharpening your words
That cut poetry
Into smaller worlds
Wherein
We, who knew defeat,
Could crawl
And, shutting out this dust,
Pretend that they were real.

From *American Poet*
January, 1943
Vol. II, No. 10

DARKEN THE ROOM

Draw the curtains in the corridors,
Where murdered beauties hang.
This one died from fear and that from hate;
This simpering dreamer knew the Judas kiss.
Not all the robust sun could warm this room,
Whose owner, even, locks it from his eyes.
For too much love, intensity of hope,
He could not go the reasonable road
Where plain-faced people spread their merchandise
And simple phrases brush the casual air.
Where mystic beauty grows,
A sullen worm may crawl along the leaf
And horrid Bluebeard, dribbling in the dark,
Cleave every dream and butcher memory's throat.
Where he is brooding, draw the shutter close.
Not even murder satisfied his kiss.

From *Three Lyric Poets*

THE INTROVERT

Now and then she is aware
Of intruders at her self's door
And slowly, furtively she creeps
Down the stairway of the mind
Fearing what her heart will find,
Whether it be ruffian, dunce or knave.
The heart is no help. It is not brave.
She pushes against the fragile door
Securities she knew before,
Defense against invading hordes
Of phrases bristling Stranger-words
Till she is sure that they have gone . . .
Traverses her mind, safe and forlorn.

From *Three Lyric Poets*

WHEN SUMMER CAME

When summer came last year
Giddy and fresh with green,
We counted the sweet clover
And tasted its scent like drink
In our mouths . . .
Till summer was over.
Now this summer's rain of blood
Has watered strange red flowers
Of flesh half-grown from earth
(For bombs are speedy planters)
To bewilder the screaming birds
Accustomed to green birth.
There are eyes grown tired of green
Must bathe their lusts in blood
And trampling the sweet clover,
But must we endure them, passive,
Aware that rhythms of green
Will return when they are over?

From *Three Lyric Poets*

LOGIC

Love is too diffuse in meanings.
I am obsessed with you
And your ways burn like acid in my blood.
Though I may be but "art object" to you
Still I could stand . . .
Let ordinary wisdom steel my thoughts
And you walled-out in stranger's harmless space
Would no more flow
Like shining waters in chaotic worlds.
Yet there is nothing in my former hours
To caution this experience of you
And though I sleep on needles
Or be drenched with rose,
I must be buffeted by madness
Till the madness blows.

From *Three Lyric Poets*

SAINT LOUIS

We arrived humbly,
Seeking a city for the captives' song,
But as we looked we said,
"This is not the place."
Cities should keep a trace of earlier time
Their own, not purchased like *objets d'art*,
To stir the memories of aged men,
Enflame the young, beguile the stranger's heart.
Yet, even the deadliest towns have egos.
Here was a stout complacent frau
With business like a rash across her face,
Once celebrated in a lusty song.
Her boulevards led nowhere, echoes came
From motor busses only,
And minstrelsy was bought on heavy terms.
We grew lonely for the sound of legendary heroes
And the places that evoke their chivalry.
Names mean only what we make them mean,
Though seers and scholars wrestle with the truth
And more than smoke is in the old man's dream.
And so LaSalle, Marquette, DeSoto, pride of Spain,
Were trade names here—discoverers lost
In the pedestrian year.
A cold wind scattered the sycamore leaves
And sent the pigeons home to their eaves.
It took us to the river, where we hardly knew
Our giant grown so thin,
Its glory muted in this cold terrain.
Still there is something in the way the air
Hangs over water anywhere
That wakens the divining sense.
We saw a town once sprawled along the docks
(Filled then with silver, furs and voyagers)
And river steamers rotting in all weather
Like rifled tombs along the glutted Nile,
An old cathedral giving its gold to the sky
And blackened buildings stamped with fleur-de-lis.
We sat a while with that swift sorcerer Time,
Who showed us how the river turned its back
When commerce like a cat took other roads.

26

The roustabouts have left their rowdy songs
In the ears of exiles.
The river long ago took Ferdinand
But lights still rise along the river's edge
At dusk as fireflies rest on marshy boughs,
And there was time for us to linger
Where something of the spirit stays
And great piazzas face the waterway
To welcome travelers on another strand.

From *Experiment*
(Reprinted in *FIRST HARVEST* of Vermont Poetry Society and
in *LYRIC LOUISIANA*, Vol. III, Louisiana State Poetry Society)

PLEA FOR REASON

I am a straw
In the blustering of events.
Unbound, facing nothing,
I was not without humor.
Straws have fallen
Under a wind
Since before the brain
Can bear to venture.
Nothing has passed
Like these black hours.
We shall not be thinned
But destroyed entirely
Unbound. Uninformed . . .
Is no time for laughter.
We, for our seed, ourselves,
Must find the compact form:
Frailty face the impending storm.

From *Three Lyric Poets*

HOUSE ON RUE ROYAL

(New Orleans)

There is a sombre grandeur in this place
That only marble mantels speak of now,
Where carven images of impish gods
Mock the ceiling's cobwebs hanging low
And footsteps framed by dust upon the floor.
And yet elusive breath, long freed,
Stirred some feeling in the room
Sensed, if not perceived,
For walls remember loveliness
Though cobweb's haggard hair
Has hushed the music
And mirthful gods have fallen fast asleep;
While we who stare with eyes across a sea,
Can never tear aside the dusty veil
Wrapped closely round a hundred changeful years.

From *American Poet*
Vol. II, No. 10
January, 1943

DEATH IN THE WOODS

Stalking on black-furred steel
The cat goes, piercing its kill
With topaz lances. Through the wood
The squirrel screams to save his blood.
Rooted to the tree he stares
At light that calls beyond his fears.
The trees, frozen footmen, witness
Now the ancient jungle kiss.
Death that harries down its foe
Must fight with breath and swiftly go
But terror gleaming beautiful
Softly rends the shuddering will.

From *The University of Kansas City Review*
   Volume XI, Number 2
   Winter, 1944

THE WORLD AND THE POET

Insistently upon the ear
Fall sounds that cause the mind to leap
Over the rounds of private stone,
To find what haunts the pulse's sleep;

To know the air the senses feel
By touching hands around a ring.
Down the silent rooms of thought
Run the songs the bodies sing!

There a lackey left to guard
The lonely house, with naught to do,
Will learn the words he scarcely knows
And later chime them, strangely new.

From *American Poet*
    (Brooklyn College)
    Volume II, Number 10
    January, 1943

IN THE FOG

The fog sifts and spreads
Over the Mississippi
Till river and sky are one grey.
Only the shacks
Sketched in black
Along the shore
Mark earth somewhere.
As if no time or thought
Were here, we float
In grey fog space . . .
Its vast uncomprehending touch
Against our face.
And the mind, too, would swim
In its cool fog
And glide forevermore
Outside the ken of fish or men
Except for dark crayoned shacks
Along the wavering shore.

The *University of Kansas City Review*
Vol. XI, Number 1
Autumn, 1944

IT IS NOW

Stranger, "Pray for Corinna Dunn,"
For whom death's terror is so real
From beyond she begs your prayers
On this old plaque of bronze and steel.
What she has done you cannot know,
Who stop for reassurance here
By marble stained with candle-glow,
Or what was fashionable that year.
Pray for your progress, but save one
For her. Your faith may be her truth
Now that ambition is undone.

From *New Mexico Quarterly Review*
  Vol. XV, No. 4
  Winter, 1945

CHANGELING

Whatever I take myself to be
(A summer heart)
In the world that seems to me
I swapped for winter's hat,
For bells, for cycles,
And rehearsed refrain
For students searching
For a summer heart.
But O, the emptiness of words
Out of the rising sun
The tuning rain.

Descant
Vol. XII, No. 4
Summer, 1968

LOUISIANA

It is not that Bienville
Came over the sea
Bringing life and lust and the melody
Of French; but that blood and bones
Of Louisiana earth
Fed a strange spirit, warm and slow,
Living in the cypress swamps,
Along the levees. Even the wise know.
It is not the green alligator
Under lush trees in a hidden place
Nor purple hyacinths across
The bayou's face.
Long forgotten language
Whispers in the ancient ear
And though we see only bearded trees
And the weird, wild birds
We sense its ghost
Across the sleeping air.

From *Prairie Schooner*
    Vol. XVIII, No. 3
    Fall, 1944

BAUDELAIRE

When was the last time
I looked in this book—
The body of my tears so long ago?
In the year of one of our wars
And now it bears the scars of peace
With yellowed pages and mottled rhyme.
My hand that holds it has changed, too,
Like the book it has life of its own,
Poised, apart from me, yet frail
As the hold of the spirit it contains,
Almost asking pity but too proud.
It speaks with a small torn nail
And a cut at the side.

You, only, the subject of words,
The master of many, have not changed.
Your picture, set in place like a stone,
But bitter and cynical, judges me
From a page, as though I, a seeker of truth,
Had made your fate
And your black eyes stare
As if I, being woman,
Were symbol of what you hate
And loved in your singular way.
Who is to judge the almost predestined poet?
You gave words to the world and
Relinquished self, whose privilege died
Before the poor flesh died.
All of us own some part of you
As we understand you.
The pathos, the evil and magic
Of words you lived are a part
Of what we, too, say secretly.
You are with us now
As we are in you.

I read your book in a cold climate
In the comfortless undeclared peace
Of now and I find I have also changed.
You are not the poet to me you were before.
You are less and more.

Southern Poetry Review
(North Carolina State University)
Vol. X, No. 1
Fall, 1969

DECISION

I once thought geometry
Might show me plainly, poetry . . .
That travel or the sciences
Had poetic alliances,
Or studies made in history gave
A key to all the rhyming brave.
Collectors spend on first editions
The awe I gave academicians.
But now I feel I was absurd
And poetry is in the word.
The ponderous, the sleek, the light,
The nimble word makes rhythms right.
And I must make with subtle tone
The structure of a laugh or moan.
I must sweep a knowing mind
And see with eyes but lately blind
Till all the vistas of a glance
Be crystallized in elegance.

American Poet
Brooklyn College
No. 12, Volume III
March, 1944

SATURDAY NIGHT AT NAPOLEON HOUSE

(New Orleans)

The "House Napoleon"
Nestled brotherhood
With airs from Traviata
Dripping insistence on a mood.
A Frenchman smiled an amorous smile,
Half-effete and guileless as a looking glass . . .
Unlike the girl-eyed boys
Who drank and chirped
Pouring cheap beer
Into rococo ribs.
"You Nordics preach," the Frenchman banged,
Diverted from his point.
No art should teach the blood.
Let music subtly steal from edge of doom
The dubious heart.
Ah!
The tunes of de Musset!
The songs of Gautier!
"You Nordics preach," and sank into his wine.
While long-eared esthetes every one
Drank beer and doted on John Donne.

From *American Poet*
Brooklyn College
Vol. III, No. 12
March, 1944

OF THE ADVISERS

Some words I read and hear,
Through the tasks and amazements,
Ring in the attentive ear.
Each master has a meaning
But the meanings clash.
The student wanting to be fair
To the sincere speakers
Finds ten commandments and a thousand spare.
None wishes to be a naive savage
Or, serenely mad, a superman
Who stares from his cold peaks;
But framed with flesh his voice
Can say no more, though sometimes less,
Than his experience or divination speaks.

From *New Mexico Quarterly Review*
Vol. XV, No. 2
Summer 1945

EACH IN HIS PLACE

Since you would take it
With you if you left it,
Stay in your ivory academe.
Some must keep the streets
And some the centuries clean.
Some must rub the past
And classify the worm
While the living build
And have what good may come.
The dust that was is safe
Further to scrutinize.
None but a friend gives
Our future dust advice.

From *New Mexico Quarterly Review*
    Vol. XV, No. 2
    Summer 1945

NEW ORLEANS AT NIGHT

Profiles of cities do not move the sky,
Yet raucous, stately, brooding faces
Can stir the pulses of the passersby.
Whether a planned and perfect city long ago
Impelled to far-flung deeds her hero-sons
I only know through legend;
But my town, whose silhouette is pocked,
Whose impudent features rise
To mock the lovely contour of the skies,
Rouses me like a lover at night
With old desires and no impulse to go.
The intimate stars of the south
Blend with her many-colored jewels,
And her traffic-husky voice
Covers disaster like a Lorelei's.

From *University of Kansas City Review*

GRAVEYARD IN CARRBORO, NORTH CAROLINA

A drizzling rain falls
On the luckless mound
Of Joseph Smith who gave
His eight year's body to the ground.

The mill-folk lie here, too,
Their juke-box motion stopped,
Immune to the imperious call
Blasting the hour, dropped

Away from strident wheels
In clifflike industries
That, toneless as a pulse,
Grind indifferent elegies.

Not that marble houses stir the dead
Whose wreaths and ribbons are forgot;
But we who mourn with pomp and artistry
Reject pine-boards and the weed-grown plot

Tangled in loneliness
The silence strafed with sound
Where dusty trees accuse
The poverty of the ground.

Over the rusty hills the day moves on
Like the hot wind that fills
The mouldering patterns of death
As tawdry as life in the careless mills.

And what of their inheritors
In the wayside Inn,
Hard as steel in the crumbling brick,
Red dust mirrored on the tightened skin?

Foes and brothers, there is something mine
In the trembling hand above the new-made bier
But the road beginning is swathed in smoke,
The tiger-eye drowned in the atmosphere.

The New Mexico Quarterly Review
Vol. XIV, No. 2
Summer, 1944

ESCAPE FROM CONFUSION

Smoke swaddles the dialectic drones
Whose queen, a stern pedantic bee,
Must Roman-think and latinize
The nomenclature of a tree.

But trees today are bombed in thought,
Events in millimeters stare.
Huddled behind defense of talk,
We seek our level in the air.

The yardsticks burn in such a heat.
The pot of history melts away,
And educated lanes of words
Are cratered by the angry day.

None could tell her, who remained,
Though it was cowardice to fly
To a gentle port of blue
Where tree-surf washes on the sky.

From *Experiment*
January, 1945

NO ONE ALONE

The vision framed with fear
Finds earth a swamp
Of strange miasmic ghosts.
What mortal sin
Paid mortal penance
In so vast a sphere?
The world a glass
Outside the early glance
Was to explore
And later earth was friend,
A power beneath the feet,
Eternity to pass.
Worlds within worlds
The adolescent eye
Found for discovery
And to be arranged.
All this was reason
Till the reason changed . . .
Shifted from season,
Out of ordinary maze,
Rhythm disrupted.
Now the burning days are here.
One alone can climb no stair
To rebuild order
From the atmosphere.

From *Experiment*
January, 1945

NEWSREEL FROM BUCHENWALD

The meaning of cruelty
Is not clearly understood
In the drawing room.
It shows itself subtly
Behind the faultless coat
And the sequin snood.
Not even in the jungle
Does the tiger
Rend the overtaken beast
For psychopathic anger.
But this deathless skeleton
Among the dead,
Plagued by insects
Now the wolves are gone,
With eyes composed of every horror tale,
Stares at a question through the visible bone.
He is its handiwork:
Cruelty is what we can become,
Who parry the ageless protest,
"What is truth?"
And lose the answers
In the drawing room.

From *New Mexico Quarterly Review*
    Vol. XV, No. 4
    Winter, 1945

FOR A POET LECTURING

When, because of revolt
Or a secret slip, will a man
Be free, wanting what he wants—
Not (when the indiscreet pulse
Slackens) what he needs
And that want long?

Moreover, I turn with a dry throat
Against wanting what is said I want.
I will keep off the grass—
Though jade under the feet is balm—
Stay in the proper zone.
In the reaping time, the wheat,
A hundred words a minute,
Whatever work I do is Theirs.

The spiritual (what is the special
Need?) is mine. No alienist,
No poet, no Chief of charts
Shall tell the want
Of the predetermined cell.

I resent, protest, reject
The universal throb
Wanting another's want:
Hearing another's voice
Cry out my need.

From *New Mexico Quarterly Review*
    Volume XV, No. 4
    Winter, 1945

ATOP CHAPEL HILL

Like marching soldiers, pines descend the hill,
Arrested by a brisk salute of air.
The town beneath veiled by the smoking mill
Seems made by distance something rare.

The new discoverers of a land explored
Bring speculation to divine the scene:
Built against chaos lies the desperate town . . .
Cool in its anarchy the unbridled green.

Saved from lost centuries this hill
Teases the milling worlds. Yet here move on
The unfathoming creatures under the still
Surface, unmolested by the moon.

A banner triumphs on a school below,
Half-hidden by a blade the cricket leaps.
The wind-sigh of the pines is sad and slow.
Indifferent as death, the ivy sleeps.

From *New Mexico Quarterly Review*
   Vol. XV, No. 4
   Winter, 1945

AFTERNOON IN CAROLINA

The boy on the bicycle mounts the tilted street
Gaining the shade, the hedge-rowed walk.
Below the hill the small shops huddle,
Reticent for all their obvious talk.

The heat now is sticky as a burr,
Only the trees have pushed it out of place—
Through which comes an aloof walker, a symbol:
England in exile with a sharper face.

A dreamer sits, weighted with heat
And noise of war (the practice planes
Roaring over the leaves like rumor winds
In Fall) immobile with imagined pains.

The dreamer patterns snares to catch his mind,
Baffled with heat, tranced by the loud
Bellies of planes, mocked by a giant dog
Which sleeps like Nero, heavy-pawed and proud.

From *New Mexico Quarterly Review*
Vol. XV, No. 4
Winter, 1945

REACTIONARY LINES

Grass, drenched with Spring,
Though fresh and new to sight,
Works old as life from a perennial heart,
Even if shrouded eyes surmise
Some untold future in the mystics of their art.
The restless coil of change
Runs steadier than we guess
Except its thousand colors
Stagger the minds too easy with their Yes.
I lived in a city scratched with time
And ran beside the faster wheels each year
But always in the framework of the old.
Such cities give back half the life they take . . .
Ancestral memories turning round a spire,
The deep voice of the river boats
Waking at night the day's confused desire.
No prophet or deliverer am I, nor you
Whose words are frozen like arrested flowers
Or whose deft action shuns the artless gaze.
We turn aside to let the living pass.

From Maine to Utah the mechanic phrase
Is introduction everywhere they.go . . .
The lonely, acquainted with all they never know.
"History" is fifty years gone by,
Simplicity the jargon of a screaming band,
With action swift and speculation slow.

Today circles like a hawk
Over the men who neither look ahead
For refuge, nor behind.
Some hold their safety
In the prison of the mind:
"Not tribal music or the minuet
Will make the hawk blind!"
And yet the skill of all,
Knowing the long chain of living—
Constancy with change—
The past remembered in the future dreamed
May bring the moment to our hand.

From *Experiment*
    Summer, 1945

THE NEED OF PEACE

To speak impulsively is to be understood
Less than a bird or some more lonely creature,
For public gestures falsify the mind.
And yet one seeks for springs of comradeship
To wash the poison of polluted times
Out of the blood,
And taps on rock and still no fountain gushes
Though the hand be bruised; while common waters
Sting the yearning throat.

"Here is the face" . . . but only seems.
No poignant meanings stare from shuttered eyes
Slaking their private thirsts their special ways.

One could be silent. But the virile want
More than cool sterility of stone.
The need of peace in utterance is real.

Humility the saints wore as a cloak
But there are ways to wear it like a shield
And gather spirit's sustenance
Among what nettles time will breed.

From *Experiment*
Winter, 1945-1946

MEMORY

Strange how this autumn evening can recall
(As an ugly twin of a fatal beauty) a night
Haunting as a myth whose names are real.
Like the black land a lake stretched far,
The wide grey sky its shore,
And with my eyes I walked distances
Immortal in darkness . . .
Calmer than peace that age has taught,
Bound as the waves beside the pier
To that ancient country of the blood
Where knowledge in the bones is fear.
Disaster makes its daily rounds now.
Cruelty is commonplace. Each face looks lonely.
All it has outruns a fear.
Yet the year turns with some bravery
And shows its colors. Children dance
On pavements of our hope.
Only when Winter waits to fall
Over the suspecting town
Some symbol, like music old and forgotten,
Wakens that sense of the somnolent dark.

From *Experiment*
Fall, 1946

THE NIGHT WAS COLD ALL NIGHT

What have I run through my mind?
The words of my comrades in life,
And the light was the flash of my pulse
As it leaped and that is most that remains.
Earlier words remain, the perfect rhyme,
The pretty adjective. These I can summon like slaves
Though their speech is of masters
Who sang for an earlier age their songs and answers.
What have I run through my mind?
The fears of my friends
Who turned and embraced their fears
As a kind of grace.
A head, full of words and fears,
Holds my slaves and signs and masters.
But awe that lives at the bone
Is steady and solitary,
Giving kinship more certain that hope can buy.
I questioned it once. I will dare no further
Its pure and remote reply.

Experiment
Vol. III, No. 2
Summer-Fall, 1947

CITY CARNIVAL

The Midway's bright balloons and blandishments
Draw swarms of black and white
That, mingling, stay distinct.
Up wooden hill, by sawdust vale
The motorcycles race. The trigger-happy
Vent their rage on target walls.
A colored countess in a velvet cape
Flaunts tinsel flowers, leaves her coach
To regiments abandoned here.
The lion has a mangy ear.
But over patched tents and the dusty ways
The calliope drops warm, nostalgic lays,
And giggling love falls over Ferris-wheels.
Here in this magic square
Sharp-etched beneath the ogres of a city,
The changelings dream of earlier homes.
At night broad beams are funneled to the sky,
But from what stale directions masses come,
Their hunger knows. The Midway
Offers stars by day and night
For them, flaring toward their primeval light.

From *New Mexico Quarterly Review*
    Vol. XVII, No. 1
    Spring, 1947

THE ALIEN

When lost to friends in some new city's maze,
The hero-mind is tranced in wonderland
To trace a steeple on another sky
To feel the glances from a foreign face
And know intensity in every casual move.
O lyric beauty of a summer vine!
O subtle singing of a stranger's street!
The friends that call the wandering heart
Find no one home. Their ghosts are quickly gone,
But when this sudden world has been explored,
A kind of night comes on.
In rooms of darkness all the old scenes live
In which those ghosts move quicker than the flesh.

New Mexico Quarterly Review
Vol. XVII, No. 1
Spring, 1947

QUESTIONS AND ANSWERS

Who sowed the seed of tortuous weeds
And throttled the garden,
Threatened the total land?
The peasant at the plow had other crops.
Lovers in dreaming time had different hopes.
The woman in the mirror wound her hair,
Wondering, "Am I my brother?"
"Am I?" answered the poet,
Who never owned a tower.
"Free," declared statistics . . .
Each different from the other.
But the eyeless growth, being poison-bred,
Never knew one from the other.

From *New Mexico Quarterly Review*
Vol. XVII, No. 1
Spring, 1947

A CITY IS A STATE OF MIND

The eastern queen, articulate and bright,
Now holds the West in fee.
Her sea is upside down,
Her gondoliers speed without song
Past maidens in those granite towers
Where conflict is not love.
Couriers of commerce with clipped words
Know all the ports.
No wonder or surprise
For caravans of sleek, exotic goods
Or perfumed lands
Startle the steadfast eyes.
When back from tedium
Of strangers' town,
Their comfort of annihilation
Covers with light
And slippers them with stone.
Meanwhile the populace
Streams to its answers
And the marvel is
No longer terror
But an attitude.

New Mexico Quarterly Review
Vol. XVII, No. 1
Spring, 1947

THE SAINT IN THE SQUARE

Old Pierre, gleaming with medals,
Blessed the smokestacks on the river
And sleeps in his parish, the drowsy Square,
Under the chartreuse sky.
Pigeons and the ships were blessed impartially
Till they and the unheeding sky
Circled into one world we could not see
Being sound and split into reality.
The saint, by his logic, barters prayers
For daily bread. The coinless leaves
Win favors free. "He is lost,"
The tourists say of a traveler to the ether.
Brown as the earth beneath him
Predictable as dawn,
A parchment scrolled with madness
Is curling in the sun.

The University of Kansas City Review
Vol. XIV, No. 3
Spring, 1948

NEW ORLEANS SUMMER EVENING

Facade gardens grow electric flowers
Brittle-blue and star-white
Dazzling the pedestrian sight.
Evening is mirrored like a girl
In window glasses.
From the theatres to ice-cream stores
Fact and fantasy are merged.
Odors from the river tease
Buccaneering memories.
St. Claude, St. Charles and *Desire*
Run beneath lines of fire.
The decor of a billiard hall
Is of a small coronation room,
Its king that old cliche called Chance.
Around the table, glittering eyes
Too tired to wonder
And to wise to think
Accept an occasional drink.
Evening goes home at last,
The stars lean down
And mingle with electric flowers.
Cities say little of days dispersed.
Here the remains of time gone. by
Stay with the living, neon-blended,
Under the warm, possessive sky.

From *The University of Kansas City Review*
Vol. XV, No. 1
Autumn, 1948

NEW ORLEANS SALON

The mirrors, gleaming with chandeliers,
Speak to eyes that understand their speech,
But the ears are soothed by Mozart, there is perfume,
And taste is wooed by delicate brandied peach.
The talk is of men and anecdotes, not methods,
In phrases like shimmering ice or bright balloons.
Every beauty is most gaily not herself
And in her eyes intriguing love blooms.
Versailles has moved to smaller Creole quarters
With sultry wit and summer most of the year.
Do not look in the mirrors for a moral.
There is no moral there.

From: *Beloit Poetry Journal*
      Vol. 1, No. 2
      Winter, 1950

PATIO NIGHT-CLUB

Under the shadow of chivalry, a lady
And gent, as sharp as any in the nightly crew,
Sit in the courtyard by synthetic fountains.
Hot stuff, as the ballads say,
And a bottle of rum for two!

Passes are not for dice alone, the lady knows,
What are the means of finding a man's intentions?
From an adjoining table, a guy with a lemon
Ogles her, a fact the lady mentions.

Here is the sign, but love and the drink are weak.
Her date declines a joust and turns to the small dance-floor.
By the light of the moon his pride shows, satisfied
That the fluff he brought is snappy and nothing more.

Beloit Poetry Journal
Vol. 1, No. 2

AUTUMN WALK

The smoke curls toward a moon that languishes.
The houses, once of neat designs,
Abstract against the flowing green,
Are stories on a pensive sky.
And our bold thought
On whispering streets,
Turns leaves of doors.
A chemistry of ritual-day
Makes colors for the evening eye;
The drama lost on time's dry wind
Arrested for the savoring.
Ourselves, at last, in all these rooms!
Sheltered from the flood of night
With fingers moving on the keys
Like living pictures in the light.

From *New Mexico Quarterly Review*
  Vol. XVII, No. 1
  Spring, 1947

CONVENTION

In the cities, cars nose in and out of pockets,
Head for small ports to satisfy the will.
By night, men stuff their ears with sound
Of female torture, canned or live,
Accompanied by accordion
Or the intense shrill of jive.
They breathe thick smoke to dull the thought of air.
Men are escaping (they do not love the ground),
From city to city, by hope or actual fare.
In bed, in death, in another time
Hangs a better climate.
Dreamers who do not understand this dream,
You are the pattern. Each city is the same.

From *New Mevico Quarterly Review*
    Volume XV, No. 4
    Winter, 1945

CREOLE ARISTOCRAT

A woman with a boat on her head
Floats down the aisle between the seas
Of French, while Gallic laughter
Sprinkles the evening with *bon mots.*
Expression marks? The eyebrows, black,
And pearls, and irony beneath the rustling clothes.
Upon what Adam-day was she born old?
What incident revives those brilliant eyes?
Whatever now is lost, no words betray
The cold dismay beneath the tired smile.
No guile will sweeten solitary pride.
Madame's chignon is perfect as before.
Her antique bracelet glitters at her side.

The *Carolina Quarterly*
Vol. 5, No. 1
Fall, 1952

IN LOVE'S TIME

Spring is no season for the stranger,
Alien, ill-favored, in love's time.
Even flowers seem distant, their burning cold,
Transformed by a witch whose subtle crime
Is unknown to the natives where kisses suffice,
Are a spell against creatures who snarl
                at the stranger.
Doves tear at the green, destroying the seed.
Lovers lean by the lilacs,
Are blind to the roses where the worms feed.
And the mind of the lonely gnaws at its pain.
It follows houndlike down torment's trail.
All beauty is bitter under the sun
Though bridal wreath is a waterfall
Of purest, whitest beginning again.

The *Colorado Quarterly*

JOURNEY INTO STONE

(For E. A. Lowe)

Stone and sorrow, heavy and light,
Are figures of our contradictions.
Buildings stare with sorrowful pride
Though vacant windows are their eyes,
And sorrow rises, step by step.
Its cornerstone was long ago
Laid in the mind by forgotten things.
Spring, the sorcerer, unveils it.
Frightened by substantial shadow,
I touch a wall's assuring side.
It does not feel as strong as sorrow
That runs like blood through all my self.
Stone dissolves and sorrow stays?
Consider the stones on weedy hummocks
Where cancelled sight and grieving stares
Are all and only in their names.
Perhaps my sorrow is not mine
But that which moves since mind began,
And stone became its truest symbol
Known in the image of sorrowing Man.

From The *Colorado Quarterly*
    Vol. II, No. 1
    Autumn, 1953

THE ANCIENT HOUSE

Our friends seemed more elusive,
The longer we searched.
Songs of strangers wafted like smoke
Over the stairs.
(And mocked by staccato ice against a glass,
Derided by taxi-horns,
Were fanciful so near to dust).
The dark stairs wound to questions
Beyond our phrase.
Guarding against a fall,
A dusty lantern flickered on the wall,
An amber eye.
Our shadows, angular on the wall,
Seemed firmly drawn,
But shadows that were not ours,
With the help of our traitor-hearts,
Reclaimed the house.
We suddenly stopped.
And for a time
Old life, new death were one . . .
As if by miracles of love
Such mysteries were known.

The *Colorado Quarterly*
Vol. II, No. 2
Autumn, 1953

PERPETUAL MOTION

Night is filled with the noise of mechanical things,
Zombies at noon that come alive by night.
With rhythm like running water
The cars glide over the street.
One suddenly shakes, coughs, and stutters,
But most of them flow
With the locust's simmering sound.
Under the wearing heat, though I slow my steps,
Bewitched creatures race that must not stop.

    The Gulf-bound train, champing and neighing wildly,
    Blinks in darkness yellow, hypnotic eyes;
    A catlike bus, swimming by narrow gutters,
    Stuffs its hungry maw with silent mice;
    And the monster of myths, out on the dark river,
    The ferry, cloaked with fog, breathes like an aging man,
    Leaves and returns though its heart bursts with the strain.

Even these walls reverberate its asthma.
Heavy slumber wakes to its heaving pain.

The *Colorado Quarterly*
Vol. II, No. 1
Autumn, 1953

LEE CIRCLE

(New Orleans, La.)

Seen from above
Cars glide on the avenue
With ease of swans.
Robert Lee's North-facing statue stares
At chaos turned to grace beneath his hill.
The motors drive to magnet window-lights
And rites of evening meals.
But in a chasm circling in the dusk
Stale, filthy flesh curls on benches.
Age lies close to evil-doers.
All own little of life but breath.
The moving hour is halted here
In a stale swamp of gathered time.
A street-car curves around the bend
Like a hero who knows his way,
And down the city's made green hill
In shadowed light I grope for mine.

From *Shenandoah*
(Washington & Lee University)
Vol. V, No. 1
Winter, 1953

Reprinted in *New York Herald Tribune*

MORNING AT SEVEN

Once when morning and roses were fresh
My mind stopped my hand in air,
As if it measured death so close
To have was loss, though irony to spare.
And at that moment even the sun
A heaven once to learning eye
Shed frailer light. On all things doom
Looked orthodox. Love burned like heresy.
All passes, yet the blood's subversive,
Its logic bullet-quick and blind.
This was the hour of our breath
And sustenance outweighed the mind.

From *Epos*
    Spring 1968

NIGHT BIOLOGY CLASS

The egg heart beat
And was a sun to me
Reflecting my heart's
Extremity.
Lonely it shone
Pulsating in its sphere
And beaming every eye
That gathered there.
The tear that trembled
On my own light's rim
Was more in fear than sorrow
For the doctor's gem:
A pounding heart,
Glassed in a cup,
An endless whim.

From *Poem*
    No. 6, July, 1969

THE UNDERWORLD

If from the hollows of the mind
Come sounds more deep and penetrating
Than those that echo on the wind,
Perhaps I should go excavating.

But I must take my lantern down
Through a dark and chilly way
For I may stumble on the stones
I put there on a thoughtless day.

And I must try to pull them up
To see why they have held so long
And learn of growth far from the sun
Where old moss and spiders cling.

Perhaps bewildered by the dark
Assailed by words so old and strange,
I'll come back silenter than stones
And blind to surface light and change.

The *Descant*
  (Texas Christian Univ.)
  (Vol. XII, No. 4
  Summer, 1968

OLD NEW ORLEANS PHARMACY

Doctor Sanders sold ice cream
And perfume labeled "Lover's Dream"

Luring the child, the simple-minded,
With many a taste and scent confounded.

He was silver and genteel.
And had the attributes of steel.

The drug-store with the rooms above
Seemed Paris. More. The black marble of

A mantelpiece, a dusty chandelier
Like a carved pendant on a monstrous ear

Rebuked the changing trade, but he fitted
His ways to theirs . . . the sly-witted,

The drunk, the base, were one to him.
Time circled under antique seraphim.

Only the mad plantation house next door
Mourned with its window eyes a lost Lenore.

Now he's gone. The houses all are going.
Beside the approaching bridge, I feel their flowing.

Nimrod
(University of Tulsa)
Vol. 12, No. 2
Winter, 1968

TENEMENT PROGRESS

The cave is square. The dusty stalactites
Falling from light bulbs tremble when cars
Rattle the long steel bones that bind the street.
Silence dribbles stone-eyed children and they stare
From stone steps veined with dirt
Like scratches that lie on arms of aged boys
Who strangle starving cats in play in alleys,
In tombs, in dank and endless night.
The silence shuffles, slinks, and then a scream
Shatters the stagnant air and everywhere
Leaps into now and here, even the fresh police.
Revolvers gleam and justice moves the soft air,
The searchlights cleave. The law
Climbs an old, forbidding stair
To rat holes where a woman hides a brute
Or drunkards cower on rags or age expires.
Curious hags and drifters sniff and stare
As luckless minions curse the climb.
"No one knows nothing," a sergeant rasps.
Sirens rage. Motors gasp. And radios bark
Another lonely crime. But from the hall
The sinister light seeps down and on the steps
Satanic children frown. They do not see
As far as they could throw the smallest stone
A church's spire, whose patron saint
The ancient serpents fled.
Symbolic finger points to lasting life.
The shanks are in the parish of the dead.

From *Pebble*
    Vol. 1, No. 1
    Autumn, 1968

GLASS UNDER GLASS

Across the sparrow's boulevards
Above their structured way,
That hawk, the eye, adventures
To apprehend the day.

Then, haunting afternoon,
Phantoms of the sky
Are almost overtaken
By the falcon eye.

Leaving channeled movement,
Unfettered sight
Finds a king's ransom
In fields of night.

Many-in-one, the eye:
Retriever from the grass,
The sifter, the deceiver,
The mind's looking glass.

Poem
No. 6, July, 1969

NEW ORLEANS NOON REMEMBERED

Laughter shatters
The saffron globe of summer air.
Angular women whose bones look wrapped
In crinkled tissue paper, shadow the walk
As they caper, and their talk
Has a rich and rhythmic sound.
Swirls of color wind their hair.

    While the sun beats down
    And the mule-bells tinkle on the street
    And compete with the trucks
    And the crippled peddler's cries,
    Their laughter rises like gulls
    Circling elusive minnows.

    The sacks they wear . . .
    Crimson, orange, rusty black
    Are signals of color
    The worn street lacks.

There are no foreigners
More foreign than these
Black old women with gleaming gold-
Brass earrings, shapeless shoes,
Moving across an ancient screen.
And the stagnant day
As they traipse to town
Closes back on itself again.

From *Poet* (Madras, India)
    January, 1969

LE RAMONEUR

(New Orleans)

Out of the play of childhood
Into the day of delight and fear
I hear the voice of the Negro "sweep"
Call *"Ramonez"* . . .
And sweep away the years.
Was it the thought of his ogre's task,
Was it the awe of the clothes he wore
Invaded night?
Black as soot from head to foot,
He conjured darkness in the light,
A dark where flame bloomed
Ghostly bright.
Ramonez, Ramonez, Ramonez
Down Rampart way . . .
Brushes and poles
Dark as his hands
Dark as the coals!
There was a piper long ago.
Children followed his haunting song;
But the call I hear
Goes down a roof
And the stove pipe hat left, anywhere
Is part of the crier
Although he breathes
In a lonely, dark and stifling air.

From *Poet* (Madras, India)
    May, 1969

JESTING PILATE?

A night biology class laboratory test
Is as funny (strange) as some of the names
Of rock bands but not for kicks.
The only one who kicks is the prof
In a sit-down kid-glove way.
We stumbled in like fools that night
And fools we were, as the grades
Told afterwards, tacked to the classroom door,
Their owners thinly veiled by initials.
The unshielded lights glared down
On microscopes, on bones laid out on paper,
On teeth from various climes and creatures,
And on platypus fur
Looking like somebody's moth-eaten coat.
Move, the doctor yelled if squinters tarried
Hoping that God would tell them whether
The crayfish was male or female.
I had done my worst when I finally came to
A chemicalized white rat, badly slivered,
And lying beside it a tiny pink thing
Looking like a miniature purse.
"Bladder," I wrote on my paper impulsively
Guessing, and finding out later I was right,
Then stared at it, so tiny,
Even pretty, and so delicate,
Following in my mind its inward service.
"O, the poor little thing," I cried
And everyone stopped . . .
"Mrs. Claudel, move" . . . the doctor ordered
In such a tone that all my fellows laughed,
More out of nerves than humor,
So I moved to a peccary's molar
That looked so much like mine.
O the arrogant, arrogant human animal!

Nimrod
(University of Tulsa)
Vol. 14, No. 2
Winter, 1970

EVENING FANTASY

As stripped of muscle as old bones,
Shaped with light against the sky,
Towers guard their warriors' cells
Below dark seas that curve so high

Sight must venture past its sphere
To scan bright islands pinned in place.
Like swimmers hurled in purling foam
We swallow fear to play in space.

Past peninsulas of green,
Cars like countless jeweled fish
Fan ceaselessly to secret caves
While the moon magnet moves the flesh.

And here in mind's own arid land
We want to toss like scraps to sea
Crumb-comforts of the narrow strand,
Swim past breakers of reality.

Beyond the sharpness of the will
That parts the waters of the night,
We long to answer choiring stars
With diapasons of delight.

From *Descant*
(Texas Christian University)
Vol. 14, No. 2
Winter, 1970

ONCE

There was a house by a persimmon tree
On a street wiped away
From a neighborhood expunged.

Yet ghosts of children play
Gathering splinters and jacks
On a gallery.
They hopscotch through a square
Or Hunt the Hare.
If bats fly down
They cover up their heads,
Leap over fences
Like hare and hound.

Their legs go like the wind
Like eyes that carry churches,
Corner store, the Levy's house
(no more)
Through falling dark.

We know where almost
All these runners ran . . .
To death the city dies
With houses gone,
Mirages under a bridge
The cars flow on
Whose living thighs are stone.

From *South*
    (Stetson University)
    Vol. 2, No. 1
    Spring, 1970

SOUTHERN SEASON

The straw bonnet
Thwarting flies and sun
Over the solemn old-maid face,
Its long ears down,
Is put away. The summer's gone.
The tinkling mule-bell
Has another sound that summoned
In the Spring the Persian look
Of jewel colors in the snowball jars
Or Roman candy and the trumpet call
Of Mardi Gras. The winter pall
Hangs in the air
Like a great fog on Chef Menteur
And slows the town
To the sad movement
Of mule-hoofs heard
On cobble stone.

The old man's head hangs down
Like the mule's ears
And grey dust powders his black skin.
The long, long street
Is captive of a spell.
It chills and calls
The lure of the impossible
Creatures moving without life.
Sparrows mark the wires.
The peddler's voice floats off
Faint and longdrawn-out
And freezing as the air
Yet whistle-clear:
"Stone coal . . . . . charcoal!"

The coal is piled so high
The tail-gate's up.
Cold eyes of houses stare
Then mirror black
And from some chant
In polar waste the echoes fall
To the measure of the cold,
Slow, clanking bell:
"COAL . . .
Charcoal . . . Stone coal . . .
S T O N E———————COAL!"

North Carolina Folklore
Vol. XIX, No. 2
March, 1971